Be empowered !

Joan Bethancourt

Tammy,

Have a marvelous, majestic birthday!

Love, Wanda
July 2010

Be Empowered!

Eat Chocolate with Breakfast

Jan Bethancourt

Janbeth Designs
P.O. Box 17192
Sugar Land, TX 77496

www.janbethdesigns.com

ISBN-13# 978-0-9815229-1-3

Artwork and Book Design — Jan Bethancourt
Project Management — Rita Mills
www.bookconnectiononline.com

The paper used in this publication meets the requirements of the American National Standard for Permanence of Paper for Printed Library Materials Z39.48-1984.

Printed in China

Dedication

With much gratitude this book is dedicated to two special women who are the essence of confidence, courage and compassion; my daughter Sarah and my mother Gerry. To my best friend and husband Bob, whose encouragement sustains me. To my wonderful son and daughter-in-law, Jim and Wendy. And, in loving memory of my step-dad Paul.

Acknowledgments

Thank you to my wonderful friends and family who have unceasingly encouraged me along the way. A very special thanks to Joanne Gochioco for saying the magic words, "I love this!", and for pointing me in the right direction. A big hug to Rita Mills who got me to press. And not least, my sincere gratitude goes to a woman who may never know how much she helped me to believe in myself. Courage becomes compassion when it inspires confidence in others. Thank you, Robin R. for making a difference.

A Chocolate Disclaimer

My lawyers said I have to do this,
so this is the way it has to be:
**If you eat too much chocolate,
don't blame me.**
In this book, chocolate is a metaphor,
except when it's not.
So, please, when you eat chocolate,
enjoy a little, not a lot.
Some people are allergic
or medically restricted.
Stay away from it,
if by chocolate you are affected.
Please, enjoy the sayings
the way they are intended;
as encouragement and inspiration with breakfast,
midday or when your day has ended.

Table of Contents

Dear Reader,

   This collection of original sayings began as e-mail messages to my daughter, Sarah, during her years of college. I encouraged her to believe in herself, to stare hardships in the eye, and to know that kindness is not only to be given, but to be graciously accepted as well.

   Chocolate, a recurring theme in my writing, is more than a rich and comforting confection; it is a metaphor for the qualities of confidence, courage and compassion.

   Life isn't always easy. It is, however, a great deal more rewarding when you have a good attitude, a genuine relationship with your Creator and a little "chocolate" with breakfast.

   My hope is that the sayings in this collection will inspire you to a greater sense of courage, self-confidence and compassion.

Be empowered!

Jan Bethancourt

Attitude

The Chocolate of Life

Attitude is an expression of how you see life:
yours and life in general.

Your Attitude Defines You

Be empowered! Eat chocolate with breakfast.

A healthy attitude is nourished by the qualities of
Confidence, courage and compassion: the chocolate of life!

Celebrate even the smallest joys in your day-to-day existence,
be it with a smile, a song, a hug or a prayer.
Celebrate!

Chocolate is the international language of women.
It speaks of confidence, courage and compassion.

Optimism inspires optimism. Be optimistic!

An occasional "pity party" is okay,
as long as you invite lots of friends and have plenty of chocolate.

Listen most closely in silence.
Look most carefully in darkness.
Touch most gently that which is fragile.
Smell most appreciatively delicate aromas.
Speak always from your heart.

Every day is trash day somewhere.
Leave your garbage by the curb.
Start over, free of all the useless stuff.

When the red wash accidentally gets tossed in with the whites,
decide pink is your new favorite color.
Accessorize accordingly!

When life has got you really down, do three things:
First, indulge in a good cry.
Second, call a close friend.
Third, take your friend along for a sinfully decadent lunch
and order chocolate for dessert.
Your problems won't go away,
but life will look so much better.

Appreciate where you have been. It takes you where you are going.

Stand in the wind and feel the breeze upon your face.
Know that your Creator has gently embraced you.

♥

Your smile will light your way.
Confidence and courage will direct you.
A joy of life will lift you when you fall.
Your love of God will bring you peace.

♥

Start each day with a healthy attitude. You will be empowered by the confidence, courage and compassion that lie within you.

Attitude

Courage

The Chocolate of Knowledge

Although courage is defined as facing difficulty without fear, true courage is facing difficulty despite your fears. Courage is what gets you through your daily life.

Chocolate Can Inspire You

With every road you walk your feet get wiser.

Identifying a problem is the greater part of solving it.

When you are having a bad day, you can improvise
with a good attitude and a little chocolate!

Don't wait for a shooting star to make a wish.

Perceive the world with all your senses.
See the old in new ways and the new with greater joy.

Embrace your future with your heart, your soul
and your whole being.

♡

Your struggles can make you stronger and wiser.
Your joys can give you hope.
If you accept them, strength, wisdom and hope
are gifts of everyday living.

It is better to think a little too well of yourself
than to doubt your value.

"What if?" won't change your past.
"What now?" will shape your future.

Heroes are ordinary people who, in a time of crisis, make extraordinary choices.

Standing up for what you believe to be right can be as simple as walking out of a situation you believe to be wrong.

Sometimes you are not appreciated because of what you stand for though secretly admired for taking a stand for what you believe in.

You are remembered not for the questions you are asked but for the answers you give.

What seems to be the most difficult of situations can become
the foundation for a positive transformation.

From a distance, a stepping stone and a stumbling
block look a lot alike. You may not be able to tell which one it is until
you are standing on it. Take the journey to discover the answer.

Seek to know your Maker, and along the journey
you will meet your truest self.

Change is inevitable. Accept the old and embrace the new.
Blend the two and that is you.

Courage empowers you to know the very best of who you are.
Begin each day with the knowledge that you can face any situation.

Courage

confidence

The Chocolate of Awareness

Confidence is described as the reliance, trust and belief in one's self.

Never Underestimate A Woman and her Chocolate!

Surprise yourself.
Set your goals beyond what you think you can achieve.
Reach farther than you can grasp.
You are more than you give yourself credit for being.

Be spontaneous!
Allow life's special times to take a shape all their own.
If you plan them too precisely in your heart or mind,
you open the possibility for disappointment.
More importantly, you could miss
the wonderful subtleties of spontaneity.

Know your heart, trust your instincts, and speak your mind.

Never doubt your power to effect change in the world around you.

Shout your dreams to the heavens,
then work like hell to make them come true!

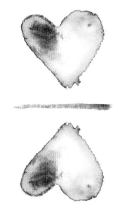

Smile at the girl in the mirror; she is your closest friend.

Instead of asking, "What is wrong with me?" ask,
"How can I be better?"

When hormones are high,
avoid making major decisions, avoid confrontation,
avoid that person who always gets on your last nerve, but
don't avoid chocolate.

You are constantly changing, growing and becoming.
Love yourself along the way.
Believe in you!

Gently exfoliate the negatives in your life that keep
the best of you from shining through.

Believe your worthy goals are attainable.

Share your imagination,
give voice to your creativity,
cultivate your talents.

Believe you are worthy of goodness.

Hope is preparing yourself to accept any outcome
while believing the best result is possible.

When you speak to God, you invite a response from God. Listen!

Your being is a triangle consisting of body, mind, and spirit.
Each part is dependant on the others for support.
Nourish, strengthen, and discover peace for each part of your being.
In that way you can face life with
confidence, courage and compassion.

Confidence empowers you to believe in yourself, to like yourself.

confidence

Compassion

The Chocolate of Kindness

Compassion is a willingness to comfort. It can be expressed in ways great or small. Compassion is a gift you offer to another, just as graciously accepting compassion is a gift.

Chocolate, When Shared,
Tastes Twice as Sweet

Make kindness a habit.

The smile you give someone may be the only one they get all day.
Give generously!

On occasion be very, very good to yourself.
Sleep late, eat chocolate with breakfast, take a bubble bath
and don't shave your legs, watch silly movies
and wear pajamas all day.

Honor your uniqueness.

Friends are there to kiss your skinned knees.
Let them. Then two people feel better!

Step outside your comfort zone. Offer a kind word
or sincere compliment to someone who would expect it least.

Listen with your ears. Hear with your heart.
Respond from your soul.

Being compassionate is a way of sharing
the Spirit that lives within you.

Your internal dialogue about external concerns
determines your overall mood.
With honesty and patience, speak kindly to yourself.

Give others a chance to succeed
before you correct the mistakes they may not make.

You can be "in control" without being controlling.

It is so much easier to keep your negative opinions to yourself
than to apologize later.

You give, someone receives. Consider the magic in that transaction. Tangible, emotional, or spiritual, your gift goes beyond the moment.

A quiet kindness speaks loudly.

Friends may not always agree on religion, politics, or guys, but they will agree to order chocolate for dessert!

Friends accept where you have been,
acknowledge who you are now,
and allow you room to grow.

Friends are like raindrops on a hot day.
They perk up your parched spirit, they help you grow,
and they flood you with an abundance of what you need.

Compassion empowers you to love the person you are.
Greet your day with an appreciation of life, of self and of others.

Compassion

Know Yourself ~ Like Yourself ~ Love Yourself

Work on an attitude that is positive

Analyze your feelings for the truth

Make your words sincere

Closely consider your decisions before acting

Keep your smile genuine

Teach your mind to be flexible

Train your body to be strong

Allow your spirit to be free

Nurture your soul to find peace

Concerning those dear to you, love unconditionally